This journal belongs to

DATE STARTED

Balboa Press books may be ordered through booksellers or by contacting:

Balboa Press
A Division of Hay House
1663 Liberty Drive
Bloomington, IN 47403
www.balboapress.com
844-682-1282

Because of the dynamic nature of the Internet, any web addresses or
links contained in this book may have changed since publication and
may no longer be valid. The views expressed in this work are solely those
of the author and do not necessarily reflect the views of the publisher,
and the publisher hereby disclaims any responsibility for them.

The author of this book does not dispense medical advice or prescribe the
use of any technique as a form of treatment for physical, emotional, or medical
problems without the advice of a physician, either directly or indirectly. The
intent of the author is only to offer information of a general nature to help
you in your quest for emotional and spiritual well-being. In the event you use
any of the information in this book for yourself, which is your constitutional
right, the author and the publisher assume no responsibility for your actions.

Any people depicted in stock imagery provided by Getty Images are
models, and such images are being used for illustrative purposes only.
Certain stock imagery © Getty Images.

Print information available on the last page.

ISBN: 978-1-9822-5668-5 (sc)
ISBN: 978-1-9822-5665-4 (hc)
ISBN: 978-1-9822-5664-7 (e)

Balboa Press rev. date: 01/29/2021

THE
MIND
HUSTLE
JOURNAL

5-MINUTE MINDSET TO MANIFEST YOUR BEST

BY RACHEL THOMAS

BALBOA.PRESS

A DIVISION OF HAY HOUSE

author

Rachel Thomas is a fifteen-year, corporate world hustler who turned to her mindset practices to create one amazing opportunity after another for herself and her family. Then she realized she could help others manifest their best lives with simple tweaks in their own mindsets. But how?

You might be wondering how this journal is different from all the others that promised to change your life. The **Mind Hustle** journal's goal is to guide you to create an easy five-minute habit of daily mindset focus while also showing you your full potential by documenting how far you've already come.

**about
this
journal**

You probably have countless journals, calendars, and planners that serve different purposes in your life. What are they giving back? What results are you getting? Do you prioritize writing in each one of them daily? You need to see some return on investment if you're going to spend your time and precious brain space on something, right? The **Mind Hustle** journal promises a place you can easily show gratitude, set your intentions for the day, document the bright points, and consider all the things that will ultimately manifest your best life. That's right, manifest! Your thoughts create your reality, and documenting those thoughts holds you accountable for your own success.

using this journal

You must remain faithful.

This is a powerful journal, but only if you believe it can work. Things might feel uncomfortable or weird at first or completely woo-woo. But seriously, what have you got to lose? Five minutes a day.

This is meant to be a daily practice, and as with anything, the more you commit, the better your results. We're not just talking about killer abs here, though. This practice has the potential to change the entire trajectory of your life for the better! Skeptical? To show you how easy it can be, I've filled in the first couple of pages to give you a good place to start.

It all begins with your intentions. I don't necessarily mean your long-term goals or biggest career ambitions; let's start with bite-size aspirations and then work our way up. What things do you want to manifest in the next ten days? A week seems too short and a month too daunting. But ten days' time seems like the Goldilocks of goal setting!

Write down things you're calling into your life, set yourself up for success, and choose intentions you know are a stretch but totally within reach. What would make you feel amazing after ten days?

Manifest Me

Personal

- Make a routine of daily meditation and mental wellness.
- Become a more peaceful, patient, and joyful mother.

Relationships

- Go on at least one date night.
- Check in on 4 friends and 2 family members.

Career

- Feel confident, accomplished, and valued at work.

Money

- Earn $500 in additional income.

Health

- Work out at least 7 of the next 10 days.
- Prioritize healthy eating.

today is when my life changes

OK, now that we've declared what's on deck for the next ten days, the fun begins. First off, this journal isn't dated, simply because we're not the judgy type, right? If you missed a day, hey, give yourself some grace and start the next. But it is important that you write the date so that you can look back and identify when those major shifts occurred in your life. Promise.

Second, document what was going on that day. What's the significance? Maybe it's your kid's fifth birthday or the day of that big client presentation that you've been working on for months. It's easier to recall the emotions that yield the best results when you can link them to a specific memory. I'm giving you an excuse to look back so that you can move forward in a direction that serves you - even if the significance is that it's just a crap-tastic day and that's all.

Once you're months into this practice, you'll start noticing amazing patterns. For example: Had a breakdown on Monday, got a promotion that Thursday!

Bet you didn't think there was significance in writing the date, huh? Just you wait ... there's plenty more magic ahead!

make gratitude your attitude

What's one thing that everyone wants more of in life? Joy!

And everything that comes along with it, of course (psst, I mean money, honey). To bring joy, you gotta think joy; you gotta get into the feeling and vibration of joy. And, baby, that all starts with gratitude.

Physically writing out what you appreciate in your life can be incredibly powerful. It can immediately change your mood or vibration. If that feels weird or sounds funny, don't worry. It doesn't have to make sense to you right now. You've probably heard the benefits of being thankful for something, but the simple ability to shift your focus to a more positive headspace will be enough to create some big results.

List three things you are grateful for. Start there. They don't have to be intense, heavy, or wildly meaningful; just write whatever you're feeling at that moment. But being grateful for the big and small makes you an energetic match for more of that.

Here's a tip: Write that you're grateful for something that you don't yet have but really, really want. You'll trick your subconscious mind into thinking you already have it and you can more easily bring that very thing into your existence. Boom - powerful!

focus on the good, no matter how small

Some might argue that the most powerful trick in manifestation is practicing gratitude. While there's a lot of truth to that, I think the ability to find bright spots in dark corners is what serves you most in your day-to-day life. Manifesting your best self has everything to do with your vibration, so you'll need a few different tools to keep that vibe high.

Let's focus our attention on optimism. What was good about your day? It's almost as if you're playing the role of your best friend, assuring yourself that it's not a bad as you think. But, what if you're so blinded by what an awful day it was that you can't see the forest for the trees?

"Sleep on it; you'll feel better in the morning."

You've heard this one before, right? What makes this daily journal practice so effective is that it gives you time to process your day, rest your mind, and look at it through a fresh lens. This makes it much easier to identify the bright points or at least the lessons learned.

"Good things happened yesterday."

Take a moment, What's a teeny-tiny good thing or absolutely amazing thing that happened? Just jot it down. Maybe you'll even be inspired to list a few extras.

take some action, baby

You can think, wish, and write about your wildest dreams, but without action, you risk staying exactly where you are. No, thank you!

What's one thing you can do to today that would get you closer to one of those ten-day Intentions? It could be reaching out to a friend you haven't spoken to in a while, applying for a job, or simply getting up early to fit in a workout.

Action can also be slowing down. Sometimes, we think that hustle is the only way to bring amazing things into our lives, but is that really how we want to spend every day - exhausted and stressed out with only a little bit more money in our pockets? No way! We want joy, bliss, relaxation, and freedom! Freedom from burnout, the grind, and feelings of overwhelm.

Those steps taken toward your intentions are called *inspired actions*. It's sometimes uncomfortable but always transformative.

Go ahead and write down what action you're taking to make this day count.

affirm it till you believe it

I'm sure you're no stranger to affirmations, but have you made them a priority in your daily practice? Do you stand in front of the mirror every morning, hands confidently on hips, proclaiming how invincible, amazing and, successful you are? Phew, me neither. But we totally should be!

Affirmations are similar to working out, eating healthily, or getting eight hours of sleep a night. We know that affirmations can have a profound impact on our health. But talking to yourself out loud and saying things that you're not quite sure you actually believe can seem a little silly or unnatural at first. The beauty of putting an affirmation in writing is that you can easily say it in your head as many times as you want before you ever have to utter a word out loud.

Put it on loop in your head; you can even set a reminder on your phone to go off a couple times a day until you can truly resonate with the message. You can use the same affirmation for ten days or mix it up, depending on what speaks to you that particular day. The important part is to say it enough times that it feels like the truth. And now that you've written it down in a safe spot, you can go back to this page when you need to hear those words in a few weeks.

Identify what works, rinse, and repeat!

I bet you were thinking that all of this was just a little basic. These are all things you've heard about but just haven't really applied in your life. But here's where we start to add a little woo-woo. You see, manifestation isn't exactly mainstream (yet). We don't learn about it at school, and it's not necessarily something you proclaim in a job interview, but that doesn't make it any less real.

show me a sign

Each one of us is on his or her own journey, and sometimes it's hard to put all your trust in the fact that things will just always work out in your favor. You're co-creating your reality. Think of your life as an experiment or as your most important group project, in which your lab partner is the universe or even God!

The steps I've mentioned up until this point have been things you could control in this experiment. But remember, you have to allow your lab partner to help too. Ask for help! Ask for a sign. Am I on the right track? Is this job offer as good as it seems? When we reach out for help, the universe or God always responds, and the easiest way is to show you!

- Choose what you want to see (e.g., a butterfly
- Choose what this sign will mean to you (e.g., take the job).
- Have faith and patience.

Because I am a tad pushy, I like to ask for two signs, one for yes and one for no. Either way, I always get my answer. The universe loves to collaborate!

it's all in the cards

When I said we were taking it a little more woo-woo, I bet this is the last thing you suspected, but get ready for the most fun you've ever had - oracle cards! Oracle cards vary by their design, message, and theme, They are cards that give direction or reveal knowledge from a divine source, God, the universe, or our highest self. Mostly, oracle cards are like different friends giving you perspectives on the same subject. They're a fun way to give meaning to your struggles and direct you towards what you need to let go of or what the future holds if you make a certain decision. You can ask any question to receive this guidance.

As part of your daily practice, I encourage you to pull a card from your favorite deck and decide how that card applies to your life or situation right now. The goal is to document this guidance as a way to look back and build your faith. Was the prediction correct? Did following the advice on the card make you feel better or more aligned? Did doing so yield results of some kind?

If you're new to oracle cards, I encourage you to check out my very own deck, **Mind Hustle**. There's no experience or interpretation needed, just quick and easy-to-understand guidance for your day. Once you select your first oracle deck, I promise you'll be hooked and might select other decks that speak to you, such as tarot or angel cards. They're all meant to be inspiring and another way to connect to your inner wisdom!

make it a habit

You knew this was coming, right? If you're making time for five minutes a day, you might as well have the space to keep track of your hard work. As with anything else, it's a lifestyle, and we're all about creating a routine that serves you, your soul, and your ultimate success. If you can make these five things a habit every day, you've seriously just collapsed your timeline to your best self. Be sure to take note of how you feel emotionally and physically at the end of ten days.

☐ Drink Water: I'm not here to micromanage your water intake, so just use your best judgment. A good place to start is 64 ounces a day.

☐ Get Moving: It doesn't have to be what you think of as exercise. You could dance to your favorite song, walk around your block, or have a full-on sweat sess. Just move it!

☐ Journaling: This one should be an easy one. Fill in your page; check the box. Boom.

☐ Meditation: Even three minutes of closing your eyes, quieting your mind, and counting your breaths can be a good place to start.

☐ Personal Development: Take a few minutes to expand your mind with insightful content. Use books, interesting articles, courses, and even podcasts - I might even recommend my own, **Hustle vs. Flow**.

Date:

Significance:

10/16/2020

Friday (finally) – Proposal Due

Thanks so much for...

1. *The fact coffee can be reheated*
2. *Healthy, happy children*
3. *My $130,000 salary for a job I love*

Good things happened yesterday...

-*Client gave great feedback on the proposal. Boss very pleased.*
-*Received a call from a recruiter.*

Action I'm taking to make this day count.

-*Updating my resume.*
-*Going to bed early – feeling a cold coming on.*

Affirmation I'm putting on loop in my head.

My success is inevitable. I am always supported, and people love to pay me for doing work that I love.

Show me a sign!

Butterfly – This new job is a good career move.
Peacock – Something even better is coming.

It's all in the cards...

Mind Hustle Deck: "Slow Your Roll"
Interpretation: I'm burning myself out at work and am not taking time to fill my own cup.

here comes the magic

How often do we intentionally look back - aside from scrolling through the camera roll on our phones? Life can get so busy that we might just be relieved that we survived another week; forget taking the time to reflect on any of our challenges or big wins.

Once you've completed ten days, go ahead and throw yourself a quick parade because showing up every day for yourself is a tremendous feat! After you've cleared the confetti, flip back through those ten days and write down all the good things that happened throughout the week on your reflection page. Felt good, huh? Now, note what you were able to manifest from your intention list and what actions brought the biggest results. Nice!

Here's where things get deep. When we take consistent action, our ego can pop up in some sneaky ways, trying to keep us playing small, staying safe.

The 10-Day Reflection pages help you make a practice of breaking through those limiting beliefs that say you're not capable, that it's selfish to want more money, or that it's not responsible for you to chase your biggest aspirations.

Call BS on those stories, re-write 'em, and prepare yourself for a massive up-level!

you ready?

Now, one last thing before we officially get started.

Are you ready? Take just a minute to collect yourself and ask these simple questions: What are you feeling in this very moment? Are you excited to start a new routine? Are you nervous to finally realize and write down what you want? Are you anxious that you'll give up on this?

Release the feelings that don't serve you and embrace those that feel good! Your first intention is starting this practice. You don't need to start at the beginning of the month or even the beginning of the week. Just start, and do so with kindness and patience. Once you complete your first ten days, you'll want to continue - if only for comparison or curiosity.

Remember: it's all your little experiment, and this journal is the one constant variable. What results will you find?

OK, it's time. You have all the tools; put those dreams on paper.

♡ Rachel

Manifest Me

INTENTIONS I'M SETTING FOR THE NEXT 10 DAYS

Personal

Relationships

Career

Money

Health

Date: Significance:

Thanks so much for ...

1.

2.

3.

Good things happened yesterday ...

Action I'm taking to make this day count:

Affirmation I'm putting on loop in my head:

Show me a sign:

It's all in the cards ...

Date:

Significance:

Thanks so much for ...

1.

2.

3.

Good things happened yesterday ...

Action I'm taking to make this day count:

Affirmation I'm putting on loop in my head:

Show me a sign:

It's all in the cards ...

Date: Significance:

Thanks so much for ...

1.

2.

3.

Good things happened yesterday ...

Action I'm taking to make this day count:

Affirmation I'm putting on loop in my head:

Show me a sign:

It's all in the cards ...

Date:

Significance:

Thanks so much for ...

1.

2.

3.

Good things happened yesterday ...

Action I'm taking to make this day count:

Affirmation I'm putting on loop in my head:

Show me a sign:

It's all in the cards ...

Date: Significance:

Thanks so much for ...

1.

2.

3.

Good things happened yesterday ...

Action I'm taking to make this day count:

Affirmation I'm putting on loop in my head:

Show me a sign:

It's all in the cards ...

Date: Significance:

Thanks so much for ...

1.

2.

3.

Good things happened yesterday ...

Action I'm taking to make this day count:

Affirmation I'm putting on loop in my head:

Show me a sign:

It's all in the cards ...

Date: Significance:

Thanks so much for ...

1.

2.

3.

Good things happened yesterday ...

Action I'm taking to make this day count:

Affirmation I'm putting on loop in my head:

Show me a sign:

It's all in the cards ...

Date:

Significance:

Thanks so much for ...

1.

2.

3.

Good things happened yesterday ...

Action I'm taking to make this day count:

Affirmation I'm putting on loop in my head:

Show me a sign:

It's all in the cards ...

Date: Significance:

Thanks so much for ...

1.

2.

3.

Good things happened yesterday ...

Action I'm taking to make this day count:

Affirmation I'm putting on loop in my head:

Show me a sign:

It's all in the cards ...

Date:

Significance:

Thanks so much for ...

1.

2.

3.

Good things happened yesterday ...

Action I'm taking to make this day count:

Affirmation I'm putting on loop in my head:

Show me a sign:

It's all in the cards ...

10-Day Reflection

Manifested from my intention list:

Actions that brought the biggest results:

Collect the good, and list 'em out:

Limiting thoughts, beliefs, or stories that came up:

Keep rolling and go manifest your best!

Your thoughts create your reality.

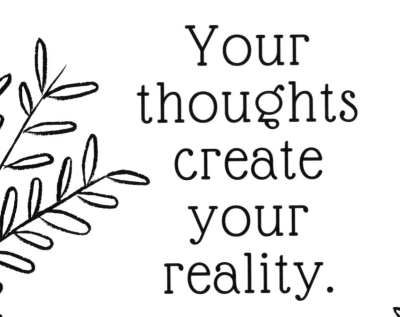

STOP WORRYING.
STOP STRESSING.
FOCUS ON WHAT
MAKES YOU AMAZING.

Manifest Me

INTENTIONS I'M SETTING FOR THE NEXT 10 DAYS

Personal

Relationships

Career

Money

Health

Date:

Significance:

Thanks so much for ...

1.

2.

3.

Good things happened yesterday ...

Action I'm taking to make this day count:

Affirmation I'm putting on loop in my head:

Show me a sign:

It's all in the cards ...

Date:

Significance:

Thanks so much for ...

1.

2.

3.

Good things happened yesterday ...

Action I'm taking to make this day count:

Affirmation I'm putting on loop in my head:

Show me a sign:

It's all in the cards ...

Date:

Significance:

Thanks so much for ...

1.

2.

3.

Good things happened yesterday ...

Action I'm taking to make this day count:

Affirmation I'm putting on loop in my head:

Show me a sign:

It's all in the cards ...

Date: Significance:

Thanks so much for ...
1.
2.
3.

Good things happened yesterday ...

Action I'm taking to make this day count:

Affirmation I'm putting on loop in my head:

Show me a sign:

It's all in the cards ...

Date:

Significance:

Thanks so much for ...

1.

2.

3.

Good things happened yesterday ...

Action I'm taking to make this day count:

Affirmation I'm putting on loop in my head:

Show me a sign:

It's all in the cards ...

Date:

Significance:

Thanks so much for ...

1.

2.

3.

Good things happened yesterday ...

Action I'm taking to make this day count:

Affirmation I'm putting on loop in my head:

Show me a sign:

It's all in the cards ...

Date:

Significance:

Thanks so much for ...

1.

2.

3.

Good things happened yesterday ...

Action I'm taking to make this day count:

Affirmation I'm putting on loop in my head:

Show me a sign:

It's all in the cards ...

Date: Significance:

Thanks so much for ...

1.

2.

3.

Good things happened yesterday ...

Action I'm taking to make this day count:

Affirmation I'm putting on loop in my head:

Show me a sign:

It's all in the cards ...

Date:

Significance:

Thanks so much for ...

1.

2.

3.

Good things happened yesterday ...

Action I'm taking to make this day count:

Affirmation I'm putting on loop in my head:

Show me a sign:

It's all in the cards ...

Date: Significance:

Thanks so much for ...

1.

2.

3.

Good things happened yesterday ...

Action I'm taking to make this day count:

Affirmation I'm putting on loop in my head:

Show me a sign:

It's all in the cards ...

10-Day Reflection

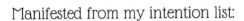

Manifested from my intention list:

Actions that brought the biggest results:

Collect the good, and list 'em out:

Limiting thoughts, beliefs, or stories that came up:

Keep rolling and go manifest your best!

Believe.

SOMEONE IS ALWAYS WORKING ON YOUR BEHALF.

Manifest Me

INTENTIONS I'M SETTING FOR THE NEXT 10 DAYS

Personal

Relationships

Career

Money

Health

Date:

Significance:

Thanks so much for ...

1.

2.

3.

Good things happened yesterday ...

Action I'm taking to make this day count:

Affirmation I'm putting on loop in my head:

Show me a sign:

It's all in the cards ...

Date: Significance:

Thanks so much for ...

1.

2.

3.

Good things happened yesterday ...

Action I'm taking to make this day count:

Affirmation I'm putting on loop in my head:

Show me a sign:

It's all in the cards ...

Date: Significance:

Thanks so much for ...

1.

2.

3.

Good things happened yesterday ...

Action I'm taking to make this day count:

Affirmation I'm putting on loop in my head:

Show me a sign:

It's all in the cards ...

Date: Significance:

Thanks so much for ...

1.

2.

3.

Good things happened yesterday ...

Action I'm taking to make this day count:

Affirmation I'm putting on loop in my head:

Show me a sign:

It's all in the cards ...

Date: Significance:

Thanks so much for ...

1.

2.

3.

Good things happened yesterday ...

Action I'm taking to make this day count:

Affirmation I'm putting on loop in my head:

Show me a sign:

It's all in the cards ...

Date: Significance:

Thanks so much for ...

1.

2.

3.

Good things happened yesterday ...

Action I'm taking to make this day count:

Affirmation I'm putting on loop in my head:

Show me a sign:

It's all in the cards ...

Date: Significance:

Thanks so much for ...

1.

2.

3.

Good things happened yesterday ...

Action I'm taking to make this day count:

Affirmation I'm putting on loop in my head:

Show me a sign:

It's all in the cards ...

Date:

Significance:

Thanks so much for ...

1.

2.

3.

Good things happened yesterday ...

Action I'm taking to make this day count:

Affirmation I'm putting on loop in my head:

Show me a sign:

It's all in the cards ...

Date: Significance:

Thanks so much for ...

1.

2.

3.

Good things happened yesterday ...

Action I'm taking to make this day count:

Affirmation I'm putting on loop in my head:

Show me a sign:

It's all in the cards ...

Date: Significance:

Thanks so much for ...

1.

2.

3.

Good things happened yesterday ...

Action I'm taking to make this day count:

Affirmation I'm putting on loop in my head:

Show me a sign:

It's all in the cards ...

10-Day Reflection

Manifested from my intention list:

Actions that brought the biggest results:

Collect the good, and list 'em out:

Limiting thoughts, beliefs, or stories that came up:

Keep rolling and go manifest your best!

Educate yo'self!

LEARN SOMETHING NEW.
READ A BOOK.
LISTEN TO A PODCAST.
ASK A QUESTION.
GO!

Manifest Me

INTENTIONS I'M SETTING FOR THE NEXT 10 DAYS

Personal

Relationships

Career

Money

Health

Date:

Significance:

Thanks so much for ...

1.

2.

3.

Good things happened yesterday ...

Action I'm taking to make this day count:

Affirmation I'm putting on loop in my head:

Show me a sign:

It's all in the cards ...

Date:

Significance:

Thanks so much for ...

1.

2.

3.

Good things happened yesterday ...

Action I'm taking to make this day count:

Affirmation I'm putting on loop in my head:

Show me a sign:

It's all in the cards ...

Date: Significance:

Thanks so much for ...

1.

2.

3.

Good things happened yesterday ...

Action I'm taking to make this day count:

Affirmation I'm putting on loop in my head:

Show me a sign:

It's all in the cards ...

Date:

Significance:

Thanks so much for ...

1.

2.

3.

Good things happened yesterday ...

Action I'm taking to make this day count:

Affirmation I'm putting on loop in my head:

Show me a sign:

It's all in the cards ...

Date:

Significance:

Thanks so much for ...

1.

2.

3.

Good things happened yesterday ...

Action I'm taking to make this day count:

Affirmation I'm putting on loop in my head:

Show me a sign:

It's all in the cards ...

Date:

Significance:

Thanks so much for ...

1.

2.

3.

Good things happened yesterday ...

Action I'm taking to make this day count:

Affirmation I'm putting on loop in my head:

Show me a sign:

It's all in the cards ...

☐ 🧴 ☐ 👟 ☐ ✏️ ☐ ☯️ ☐ 📖

Date: Significance:

Thanks so much for ...

1.

2.

3.

Good things happened yesterday ...

Action I'm taking to make this day count:

Affirmation I'm putting on loop in my head:

Show me a sign:

It's all in the cards ...

Date: Significance:

Thanks so much for ...

1.

2.

3.

Good things happened yesterday ...

Action I'm taking to make this day count:

Affirmation I'm putting on loop in my head:

Show me a sign:

It's all in the cards ...

Date:

Significance:

Thanks so much for ...

1.

2.

3.

Good things happened yesterday ...

Action I'm taking to make this day count:

Affirmation I'm putting on loop in my head:

Show me a sign:

It's all in the cards ...

Date: Significance:

Thanks so much for ...

1.

2.

3.

Good things happened yesterday ...

Action I'm taking to make this day count:

Affirmation I'm putting on loop in my head:

Show me a sign:

It's all in the cards ...

10-Day Reflection

LOOK BACK, WORK THROUGH, MOVE FORWARD.

Manifested from my intention list:

Actions that brought the biggest results:

Collect the good, and list 'em out:

Limiting thoughts, beliefs, or stories that came up:

Keep rolling and go manifest your best!

Know this: you are worthy.

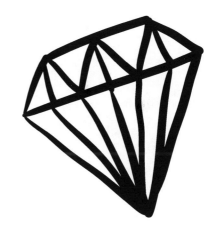

**YOU ARE WORTHY OF
LOVE, ACCEPTANCE, JOY,
RESPECT AND
MONEY, HONEY!**

Manifest Me

INTENTIONS I'M SETTING FOR THE NEXT 10 DAYS

Personal

Relationships

Career

Money

Health

Date:

Significance:

Thanks so much for ...

1.

2.

3.

Good things happened yesterday ...

Action I'm taking to make this day count:

Affirmation I'm putting on loop in my head:

Show me a sign:

It's all in the cards ...

Date: Significance:

Thanks so much for ...

1.

2.

3.

Good things happened yesterday ...

Action I'm taking to make this day count:

Affirmation I'm putting on loop in my head:

Show me a sign:

It's all in the cards ...

Date: _____   Significance: _____

Thanks so much for ...

1.

2.

3.

Good things happened yesterday ...

Action I'm taking to make this day count:

Affirmation I'm putting on loop in my head:

Show me a sign:

It's all in the cards ...

☐ 🥤   ☐ 👟   ☐ ✏️   ☐ ☯️   ☐ 📖

Date: Significance:

Thanks so much for ...

1.

2.

3.

Good things happened yesterday ...

Action I'm taking to make this day count:

Affirmation I'm putting on loop in my head:

Show me a sign:

It's all in the cards ...

Date:

Significance:

Thanks so much for ...

1.

2.

3.

Good things happened yesterday ...

Action I'm taking to make this day count:

Affirmation I'm putting on loop in my head:

Show me a sign:

It's all in the cards ...

Date:

Significance:

Thanks so much for ...

1.

2.

3.

Good things happened yesterday ...

Action I'm taking to make this day count:

Affirmation I'm putting on loop in my head:

Show me a sign:

It's all in the cards ...

Date:

Significance:

Thanks so much for ...

1.

2.

3.

Good things happened yesterday ...

Action I'm taking to make this day count:

Affirmation I'm putting on loop in my head:

Show me a sign:

It's all in the cards ...

Date: Significance:

Thanks so much for …

1.

2.

3.

Good things happened yesterday …

Action I'm taking to make this day count:

Affirmation I'm putting on loop in my head:

Show me a sign:

It's all in the cards …

Date: Significance:

Thanks so much for ...

1.

2.

3.

Good things happened yesterday ...

Action I'm taking to make this day count:

Affirmation I'm putting on loop in my head:

Show me a sign:

It's all in the cards ...

Date:

Significance:

Thanks so much for ...

1.

2.

3.

Good things happened yesterday ...

Action I'm taking to make this day count:

Affirmation I'm putting on loop in my head:

Show me a sign:

It's all in the cards ...

10-Day Reflection

LOOK BACK, WORK THROUGH, MOVE FORWARD.

Manifested from my intention list:

Actions that brought the biggest results:

Collect the good, and list 'em out:

Limiting thoughts, beliefs, or stories that came up:

Keep rolling and go manifest your best!

Take action.

TAKE A SMALL STEP TOWARD WHAT YOU WANT YOUR LIFE TO LOOK LIKE.

Manifest Me

INTENTIONS I'M SETTING FOR THE NEXT 10 DAYS

Personal

Relationships

Career

Money

Health

Date: Significance:

Thanks so much for ...

1.

2.

3.

Good things happened yesterday ...

Action I'm taking to make this day count:

Affirmation I'm putting on loop in my head:

Show me a sign:

It's all in the cards ...

Date: Significance:

Thanks so much for ...

1.

2.

3.

Good things happened yesterday ...

Action I'm taking to make this day count:

Affirmation I'm putting on loop in my head:

Show me a sign:

It's all in the cards ...

Date: Significance:

Thanks so much for ...

1.

2.

3.

Good things happened yesterday ...

Action I'm taking to make this day count:

Affirmation I'm putting on loop in my head:

Show me a sign:

It's all in the cards ...

Date: Significance:

Thanks so much for ...

1.

2.

3.

Good things happened yesterday ...

Action I'm taking to make this day count:

Affirmation I'm putting on loop in my head:

Show me a sign:

It's all in the cards ...

Date: Significance:

Thanks so much for ...

1.

2.

3.

Good things happened yesterday ...

Action I'm taking to make this day count:

Affirmation I'm putting on loop in my head:

Show me a sign:

It's all in the cards ...

Date: Significance:

Thanks so much for ...

1.

2.

3.

Good things happened yesterday ...

Action I'm taking to make this day count:

Affirmation I'm putting on loop in my head:

Show me a sign:

It's all in the cards ...

Date: Significance:

Thanks so much for ...

1.

2.

3.

Good things happened yesterday ...

Action I'm taking to make this day count:

Affirmation I'm putting on loop in my head:

Show me a sign:

It's all in the cards ...

Date: Significance:

Thanks so much for ...

1.

2.

3.

Good things happened yesterday ...

Action I'm taking to make this day count:

Affirmation I'm putting on loop in my head:

Show me a sign:

It's all in the cards ...

Date: Significance:

Thanks so much for ...

1.

2.

3.

Good things happened yesterday ...

Action I'm taking to make this day count:

Affirmation I'm putting on loop in my head:

Show me a sign:

It's all in the cards ...

Date: Significance:

Thanks so much for ...

1.

2.

3.

Good things happened yesterday ...

Action I'm taking to make this day count:

Affirmation I'm putting on loop in my head:

Show me a sign:

It's all in the cards ...

10-Day Reflection

Manifested from my intention list:

Actions that brought the biggest results:

Collect the good, and list 'em out:

Limiting thoughts, beliefs, or stories that came up:

Keep rolling and go manifest your best!

Serve others.

ASK FRIENDS HOW
THEY'RE DOING, BRING
SOMEONE COFFEE,
DROP EVERYTHING AND
HELP SOMEONE.

Manifest Me

INTENTIONS I'M SETTING FOR THE NEXT 10 DAYS

Personal

Relationships

Career

Money

Health

Date: Significance:

Thanks so much for ...

1.

2.

3.

Good things happened yesterday ...

Action I'm taking to make this day count:

Affirmation I'm putting on loop in my head:

Show me a sign:

It's all in the cards ...

☐ 🖊 ☐ 👟 ☐ ✏️ ☐ ☯ ☐ 📖

Date: Significance:

Thanks so much for ...

1.

2.

3.

Good things happened yesterday ...

Action I'm taking to make this day count:

Affirmation I'm putting on loop in my head:

Show me a sign:

It's all in the cards ...

Date: Significance:

Thanks so much for ...

1.

2.

3.

Good things happened yesterday ...

Action I'm taking to make this day count:

Affirmation I'm putting on loop in my head:

Show me a sign:

It's all in the cards ...

Date: Significance:

Thanks so much for ...

1.

2.

3.

Good things happened yesterday ...

Action I'm taking to make this day count:

Affirmation I'm putting on loop in my head:

Show me a sign:

It's all in the cards ...

Date:

Significance:

Thanks so much for ...

1.

2.

3.

Good things happened yesterday ...

Action I'm taking to make this day count:

Affirmation I'm putting on loop in my head:

Show me a sign:

It's all in the cards ...

Date:

Significance:

Thanks so much for ...

1.

2.

3.

Good things happened yesterday ...

Action I'm taking to make this day count:

Affirmation I'm putting on loop in my head:

Show me a sign:

It's all in the cards ...

Date: Significance:

Thanks so much for ...

1.

2.

3.

Good things happened yesterday ...

Action I'm taking to make this day count:

Affirmation I'm putting on loop in my head:

Show me a sign:

It's all in the cards ...

Date: Significance:

Thanks so much for ...

1.

2.

3.

Good things happened yesterday ...

Action I'm taking to make this day count:

Affirmation I'm putting on loop in my head:

Show me a sign:

It's all in the cards ...

Date:

Significance:

Thanks so much for ...

1.

2.

3.

Good things happened yesterday ...

Action I'm taking to make this day count:

Affirmation I'm putting on loop in my head:

Show me a sign:

It's all in the cards ...

Date: Significance:

Thanks so much for ...

1.

2.

3.

Good things happened yesterday ...

Action I'm taking to make this day count:

Affirmation I'm putting on loop in my head:

Show me a sign:

It's all in the cards ...

10-Day Reflection

Manifested from my intention list:

Actions that brought the biggest results:

Collect the good, and list 'em out:

Limiting thoughts, beliefs, or stories that came up:

Keep rolling and go manifest your best!

Surrender your fears today.

DO THEY SERVE YOU?
ARE THEY TRUE?
WORK THROUGH
THOSE STORIES!

Manifest Me

INTENTIONS I'M SETTING FOR THE NEXT 10 DAYS

Personal

Relationships

Career

Money

Health

Date:

Significance:

Thanks so much for …

1.

2.

3.

Good things happened yesterday …

Action I'm taking to make this day count:

Affirmation I'm putting on loop in my head:

Show me a sign:

It's all in the cards …

Date: Significance:

Thanks so much for ...

1.

2.

3.

Good things happened yesterday ...

Action I'm taking to make this day count:

Affirmation I'm putting on loop in my head:

Show me a sign:

It's all in the cards ...

Date: _____ Significance: _____

Thanks so much for ...

1.

2.

3.

Good things happened yesterday ...

Action I'm taking to make this day count:

Affirmation I'm putting on loop in my head:

Show me a sign:

It's all in the cards ...

Date: Significance:

Thanks so much for ...

1.

2.

3.

Good things happened yesterday ...

Action I'm taking to make this day count:

Affirmation I'm putting on loop in my head:

Show me a sign:

It's all in the cards ...

Date:

Significance:

Thanks so much for ...

1.

2.

3.

Good things happened yesterday ...

Action I'm taking to make this day count:

Affirmation I'm putting on loop in my head:

Show me a sign:

It's all in the cards ...

Date: Significance:

Thanks so much for ...

1.

2.

3.

Good things happened yesterday ...

Action I'm taking to make this day count:

Affirmation I'm putting on loop in my head:

Show me a sign:

It's all in the cards ...

Date:

Significance:

Thanks so much for ...

1.

2.

3.

Good things happened yesterday ...

Action I'm taking to make this day count:

Affirmation I'm putting on loop in my head:

Show me a sign:

It's all in the cards ...

Date:

Significance:

Thanks so much for ...

1.

2.

3.

Good things happened yesterday ...

Action I'm taking to make this day count:

Affirmation I'm putting on loop in my head:

Show me a sign:

It's all in the cards ...

Date: Significance:

Thanks so much for ...

1.

2.

3.

Good things happened yesterday ...

Action I'm taking to make this day count:

Affirmation I'm putting on loop in my head:

Show me a sign:

It's all in the cards ...

Date: Significance:

Thanks so much for ...

1.

2.

3.

Good things happened yesterday ...

Action I'm taking to make this day count:

Affirmation I'm putting on loop in my head:

Show me a sign:

It's all in the cards ...

10-Day Reflection

LOOK BACK, WORK THROUGH, MOVE FORWARD.

Manifested from my intention list:

Actions that brought the biggest results:

Collect the good, and list 'em out:

Limiting thoughts, beliefs, or stories that came up:

Keep rolling and go manifest your best!

It's OK to not be OK.

FIND PEACE KNOWING
THAT YOU HAVE THE
CAPABILITY TO MOVE
THROUGH THIS.

Manifest Me

INTENTIONS I'M SETTING FOR THE NEXT 10 DAYS

Personal

Relationships

Career

Money

Health

Date:

Significance:

Thanks so much for ...

1.

2.

3.

Good things happened yesterday ...

Action I'm taking to make this day count:

Affirmation I'm putting on loop in my head:

Show me a sign:

It's all in the cards ...

Date:

Significance:

Thanks so much for ...

1.

2.

3.

Good things happened yesterday ...

Action I'm taking to make this day count:

Affirmation I'm putting on loop in my head:

Show me a sign:

It's all in the cards ...

Date: Significance:

Thanks so much for ...

1.

2.

3.

Good things happened yesterday ...

Action I'm taking to make this day count:

Affirmation I'm putting on loop in my head:

Show me a sign:

It's all in the cards ...

Date: _____   Significance: _____

Thanks so much for ...

1.

2.

3.

Good things happened yesterday ...

Action I'm taking to make this day count:

Affirmation I'm putting on loop in my head:

Show me a sign:

It's all in the cards ...

Date: Significance:

Thanks so much for ...

1.

2.

3.

Good things happened yesterday ...

Action I'm taking to make this day count:

Affirmation I'm putting on loop in my head:

Show me a sign:

It's all in the cards ...

Date: Significance:

Thanks so much for ...

1.

2.

3.

Good things happened yesterday ...

Action I'm taking to make this day count:

Affirmation I'm putting on loop in my head:

Show me a sign:

It's all in the cards ...

Date: Significance:

Thanks so much for ...

1.

2.

3.

Good things happened yesterday ...

Action I'm taking to make this day count:

Affirmation I'm putting on loop in my head:

Show me a sign:

It's all in the cards ...

Date: Significance:

Thanks so much for ...

1.

2.

3.

Good things happened yesterday ...

Action I'm taking to make this day count:

Affirmation I'm putting on loop in my head:

Show me a sign:

It's all in the cards ...

Date:

Significance:

Thanks so much for ...

1.

2.

3.

Good things happened yesterday ...

Action I'm taking to make this day count:

Affirmation I'm putting on loop in my head:

Show me a sign:

It's all in the cards ...

Date: Significance:

Thanks so much for ...

1.

2.

3.

Good things happened yesterday ...

Action I'm taking to make this day count:

Affirmation I'm putting on loop in my head:

Show me a sign:

It's all in the cards ...

10-Day Reflection

LOOK BACK, WORK THROUGH, MOVE FORWARD.

Manifested from my intention list:

Actions that brought the biggest results:

Collect the good, and list 'em out:

Limiting thoughts, beliefs, or stories that came up:

Keep rolling and go manifest your best!

You are exactly what people need.

SHINE ON, MY FRIEND!

Manifest Me

INTENTIONS I'M SETTING FOR THE NEXT 10 DAYS

Personal

Relationships

Career

Money

Health

Date: Significance:

Thanks so much for ...

1.

2.

3.

Good things happened yesterday ...

Action I'm taking to make this day count:

Affirmation I'm putting on loop in my head:

Show me a sign:

It's all in the cards ...

Date:

Significance:

Thanks so much for ...

1.

2.

3.

Good things happened yesterday ...

Action I'm taking to make this day count:

Affirmation I'm putting on loop in my head:

Show me a sign:

It's all in the cards ...

Date:

Significance:

Thanks so much for ...

1.

2.

3.

Good things happened yesterday ...

Action I'm taking to make this day count:

Affirmation I'm putting on loop in my head:

Show me a sign:

It's all in the cards ...

Date: Significance:

Thanks so much for ...

1.

2.

3.

Good things happened yesterday ...

Action I'm taking to make this day count:

Affirmation I'm putting on loop in my head:

Show me a sign:

It's all in the cards ...

Date:

Significance:

Thanks so much for ...

1.

2.

3.

Good things happened yesterday ...

Action I'm taking to make this day count:

Affirmation I'm putting on loop in my head:

Show me a sign:

It's all in the cards ...

Date:

Significance:

Thanks so much for ...

1.

2.

3.

Good things happened yesterday ...

Action I'm taking to make this day count:

Affirmation I'm putting on loop in my head:

Show me a sign:

It's all in the cards ...

Date: Significance:

Thanks so much for ...

1.

2.

3.

Good things happened yesterday ...

Action I'm taking to make this day count:

Affirmation I'm putting on loop in my head:

Show me a sign:

It's all in the cards ...

Date:

Significance:

Thanks so much for ...

1.

2.

3.

Good things happened yesterday ...

Action I'm taking to make this day count:

Affirmation I'm putting on loop in my head:

Show me a sign:

It's all in the cards ...

Date: Significance:

Thanks so much for ...

1.

2.

3.

Good things happened yesterday ...

Action I'm taking to make this day count:

Affirmation I'm putting on loop in my head:

Show me a sign:

It's all in the cards ...

Date: Significance:

Thanks so much for ...

1.

2.

3.

Good things happened yesterday ...

Action I'm taking to make this day count:

Affirmation I'm putting on loop in my head:

Show me a sign:

It's all in the cards ...

10-Day Reflection

Manifested from my intention list:

Actions that brought the biggest results:

Collect the good, and list 'em out:

Limiting thoughts, beliefs, or stories that came up:

Keep rolling and go manifest your best!

There's more where that came from!

**THERE IS ALWAYS
ENOUGH TO GO
AROUND.**

Manifest Me

INTENTIONS I'M SETTING FOR THE NEXT 10 DAYS

Personal

Relationships

Career

Money

Health

Date: Significance:

Thanks so much for ...

1.

2.

3.

Good things happened yesterday ...

Action I'm taking to make this day count:

Affirmation I'm putting on loop in my head:

Show me a sign:

It's all in the cards ...

Date:

Significance:

Thanks so much for ...

1.

2.

3.

Good things happened yesterday ...

Action I'm taking to make this day count:

Affirmation I'm putting on loop in my head:

Show me a sign:

It's all in the cards ...

Date: Significance:

Thanks so much for ...

1.

2.

3.

Good things happened yesterday ...

Action I'm taking to make this day count:

Affirmation I'm putting on loop in my head:

Show me a sign:

It's all in the cards ...

Date: Significance:

Thanks so much for ...

1.

2.

3.

Good things happened yesterday ...

Action I'm taking to make this day count:

Affirmation I'm putting on loop in my head:

Show me a sign:

It's all in the cards ...

Date:

Significance:

Thanks so much for ...

1.

2.

3.

Good things happened yesterday ...

Action I'm taking to make this day count:

Affirmation I'm putting on loop in my head:

Show me a sign:

It's all in the cards ...

☐ 🧴   ☐ 👟   ☐ ✏️   ☐ ☯️   ☐ 📖

Date: Significance:

Thanks so much for ...

1.

2.

3.

Good things happened yesterday ...

Action I'm taking to make this day count:

Affirmation I'm putting on loop in my head:

Show me a sign:

It's all in the cards ...

Date: Significance:

Thanks so much for …

1.

2.

3.

Good things happened yesterday …

Action I'm taking to make this day count:

Affirmation I'm putting on loop in my head:

Show me a sign:

It's all in the cards …

Date:

Significance:

Thanks so much for ...

1.

2.

3.

Good things happened yesterday ...

Action I'm taking to make this day count:

Affirmation I'm putting on loop in my head:

Show me a sign:

It's all in the cards ...

Date:

Significance:

Thanks so much for ...

1.

2.

3.

Good things happened yesterday ...

Action I'm taking to make this day count:

Affirmation I'm putting on loop in my head:

Show me a sign:

It's all in the cards ...

Date: _____   Significance: _____

Thanks so much for ...

1.

2.

3.

Good things happened yesterday ...

Action I'm taking to make this day count:

Affirmation I'm putting on loop in my head:

Show me a sign:

It's all in the cards ...

☐ 🧴   ☐ 👟   ☐ ✏️   ☐ ☯️   ☐ 📖

10-Day Reflection

LOOK BACK, WORK THROUGH, MOVE FORWARD.

Manifested from my intention list:

Actions that brought the biggest results:

Collect the good, and list 'em out:

Limiting thoughts, beliefs, or stories that came up:

Keep rolling and go manifest your best!

Feel
excited.

**THAT'S WHAT YOUR
DREAM LIFE FEELS
LIKE. YOU'RE
WELCOME.**

Manifest Me

INTENTIONS I'M SETTING FOR THE NEXT 10 DAYS

Personal

Relationships

Career

Money

Health

Date: Significance:

Thanks so much for ...

1.

2.

3.

Good things happened yesterday ...

Action I'm taking to make this day count:

Affirmation I'm putting on loop in my head:

Show me a sign:

It's all in the cards ...

☐ 🧴   ☐ 👟   ☐ ✏️   ☐ ☯️   ☐ 📖

Date: Significance:

Thanks so much for ...

1.

2.

3.

Good things happened yesterday ...

Action I'm taking to make this day count:

Affirmation I'm putting on loop in my head:

Show me a sign:

It's all in the cards ...

☐ 🧴   ☐ 👟   ☐ ✏️   ☐ ☯️   ☐ 📖

Date: Significance:

Thanks so much for ...

1.

2.

3.

Good things happened yesterday ...

Action I'm taking to make this day count:

Affirmation I'm putting on loop in my head:

Show me a sign:

It's all in the cards ...

Date: Significance:

Thanks so much for ...

1.

2.

3.

Good things happened yesterday ...

Action I'm taking to make this day count:

Affirmation I'm putting on loop in my head:

Show me a sign:

It's all in the cards ...

☐ 🧴   ☐ 👟   ☐ ✏️   ☐ ☯️   ☐ 📖

Date: Significance:

Thanks so much for ...

1.

2.

3.

Good things happened yesterday ...

Action I'm taking to make this day count:

Affirmation I'm putting on loop in my head:

Show me a sign:

It's all in the cards ...

Date: Significance:

Thanks so much for ...

1.

2.

3.

Good things happened yesterday ...

Action I'm taking to make this day count:

Affirmation I'm putting on loop in my head:

Show me a sign:

It's all in the cards ...

Date: Significance:

Thanks so much for ...

1.

2.

3.

Good things happened yesterday ...

Action I'm taking to make this day count:

Affirmation I'm putting on loop in my head:

Show me a sign:

It's all in the cards ...

☐ 🖊   ☐ 👟   ☐ ✏️   ☐ ☯   ☐ 📖

Date: Significance:

Thanks so much for ...

1.

2.

3.

Good things happened yesterday ...

Action I'm taking to make this day count:

Affirmation I'm putting on loop in my head:

Show me a sign:

It's all in the cards ...

Date: Significance:

Thanks so much for ...

1.

2.

3.

Good things happened yesterday ...

Action I'm taking to make this day count:

Affirmation I'm putting on loop in my head:

Show me a sign:

It's all in the cards ...

Date: Significance:

Thanks so much for ...

1.

2.

3.

Good things happened yesterday ...

Action I'm taking to make this day count:

Affirmation I'm putting on loop in my head:

Show me a sign:

It's all in the cards ...

10-Day Reflection

Manifested from my intention list:

Actions that brought the biggest results:

Collect the good, and list 'em out:

Limiting thoughts, beliefs, or stories that came up:

Keep rolling and go manifest your best!

Remind yourself how far you've come.

DANG, YOU DID ALL THAT? IMPRESSIVE!

Manifest Me

INTENTIONS I'M SETTING FOR THE NEXT 10 DAYS

Personal

Relationships

Career

Money

Health

Date: Significance:

Thanks so much for ...

1.

2.

3.

Good things happened yesterday ...

Action I'm taking to make this day count:

Affirmation I'm putting on loop in my head:

Show me a sign:

It's all in the cards ...

Date: Significance:

Thanks so much for ...

1.

2.

3.

Good things happened yesterday ...

Action I'm taking to make this day count:

Affirmation I'm putting on loop in my head:

Show me a sign:

It's all in the cards ...

Date: Significance:

Thanks so much for ...

1.

2.

3.

Good things happened yesterday ...

Action I'm taking to make this day count:

Affirmation I'm putting on loop in my head:

Show me a sign:

It's all in the cards ...

Date: Significance:

Thanks so much for ...

1.

2.

3.

Good things happened yesterday ...

Action I'm taking to make this day count:

Affirmation I'm putting on loop in my head:

Show me a sign:

It's all in the cards ...

Date: Significance:

Thanks so much for ...

1.

2.

3.

Good things happened yesterday ...

Action I'm taking to make this day count:

Affirmation I'm putting on loop in my head:

Show me a sign:

It's all in the cards ...

Date: _____ Significance: _____

Thanks so much for ...

1.

2.

3.

Good things happened yesterday ...

Action I'm taking to make this day count:

Affirmation I'm putting on loop in my head:

Show me a sign:

It's all in the cards ...

Date:

Significance:

Thanks so much for ...

1.

2.

3.

Good things happened yesterday ...

Action I'm taking to make this day count:

Affirmation I'm putting on loop in my head:

Show me a sign:

It's all in the cards ...

Date: Significance:

Thanks so much for ...

1.

2.

3.

Good things happened yesterday ...

Action I'm taking to make this day count:

Affirmation I'm putting on loop in my head:

Show me a sign:

It's all in the cards ...

☐ 🧴   ☐ 👟   ☐ ✏️   ☐ ☯️   ☐ 📖

Date: Significance:

Thanks so much for ...

1.

2.

3.

Good things happened yesterday ...

Action I'm taking to make this day count:

Affirmation I'm putting on loop in my head:

Show me a sign:

It's all in the cards ...

Date:

Significance:

Thanks so much for ...

1.

2.

3.

Good things happened yesterday ...

Action I'm taking to make this day count:

Affirmation I'm putting on loop in my head:

Show me a sign:

It's all in the cards ...

Date:

Significance:

Thanks so much for ...

1.

2.

3.

Good things happened yesterday ...

Action I'm taking to make this day count:

Affirmation I'm putting on loop in my head:

Show me a sign:

It's all in the cards ...

Have some fun.

OH, HELLO! WHO IS THIS
EASY-BREEZY SELF?
YOU CUTE.

Manifest Me

INTENTIONS I'M SETTING FOR THE NEXT 10 DAYS

Personal

Relationships

Career

Money

Health

Date: Significance:

Thanks so much for ...

1.

2.

3.

Good things happened yesterday ...

Action I'm taking to make this day count:

Affirmation I'm putting on loop in my head:

Show me a sign:

It's all in the cards ...

Date: Significance:

Thanks so much for ...

1.

2.

3.

Good things happened yesterday ...

Action I'm taking to make this day count:

Affirmation I'm putting on loop in my head:

Show me a sign:

It's all in the cards ...

Date:

Significance:

Thanks so much for ...

1.

2.

3.

Good things happened yesterday ...

Action I'm taking to make this day count:

Affirmation I'm putting on loop in my head:

Show me a sign:

It's all in the cards ...

Date: Significance:

Thanks so much for ...

1.

2.

3.

Good things happened yesterday ...

Action I'm taking to make this day count:

Affirmation I'm putting on loop in my head:

Show me a sign:

It's all in the cards ...

Date: Significance:

Thanks so much for ...

1.

2.

3.

Good things happened yesterday ...

Action I'm taking to make this day count:

Affirmation I'm putting on loop in my head:

Show me a sign:

It's all in the cards ...

Date:

Significance:

Thanks so much for ...

1.

2.

3.

Good things happened yesterday ...

Action I'm taking to make this day count:

Affirmation I'm putting on loop in my head:

Show me a sign:

It's all in the cards ...

☐ 🧴   ☐ 👟   ☐ ✏️   ☐ ☯️   ☐ 📖

Date: Significance:

Thanks so much for ...

1.

2.

3.

Good things happened yesterday ...

Action I'm taking to make this day count:

Affirmation I'm putting on loop in my head:

Show me a sign:

It's all in the cards ...

Date: Significance:

Thanks so much for ...

1.

2.

3.

Good things happened yesterday ...

Action I'm taking to make this day count:

Affirmation I'm putting on loop in my head:

Show me a sign:

It's all in the cards ...

☐ 🧴   ☐ 👟   ☐ ✏️   ☐ ☯️   ☐ 📖

Date:

Significance:

Thanks so much for ...

1.

2.

3.

Good things happened yesterday ...

Action I'm taking to make this day count:

Affirmation I'm putting on loop in my head:

Show me a sign:

It's all in the cards ...

Date: Significance:

Thanks so much for ...

1.

2.

3.

Good things happened yesterday ...

Action I'm taking to make this day count:

Affirmation I'm putting on loop in my head:

Show me a sign:

It's all in the cards ...

10-Day Reflection

Manifested from my intention list:

Actions that brought the biggest results:

Collect the good, and list 'em out:

Limiting thoughts, beliefs, or stories that came up:

Keep rolling and go manifest your best!

Time to go with the flow and slow your roll.

SIT BACK, AND LET IT
ALL COME TO YOU!

Manifest Me

INTENTIONS I'M SETTING FOR THE NEXT 10 DAYS

Personal

Relationships

Career

Money

Health

Date: Significance:

Thanks so much for ...

1.

2.

3.

Good things happened yesterday ...

Action I'm taking to make this day count:

Affirmation I'm putting on loop in my head:

Show me a sign:

It's all in the cards ...

Date: Significance:

Thanks so much for ...

1.

2.

3.

Good things happened yesterday ...

Action I'm taking to make this day count:

Affirmation I'm putting on loop in my head:

Show me a sign:

It's all in the cards ...

Date:

Significance:

Thanks so much for ...

1.

2.

3.

Good things happened yesterday ...

Action I'm taking to make this day count:

Affirmation I'm putting on loop in my head:

Show me a sign:

It's all in the cards ...

Date: Significance:

Thanks so much for ...

1.

2.

3.

Good things happened yesterday ...

Action I'm taking to make this day count:

Affirmation I'm putting on loop in my head:

Show me a sign:

It's all in the cards ...

Date: Significance:

Thanks so much for ...

1.

2.

3.

Good things happened yesterday ...

Action I'm taking to make this day count:

Affirmation I'm putting on loop in my head:

Show me a sign:

It's all in the cards ...

☐ ✒   ☐ 👟   ☐ ✏   ☐ ☯   ☐ 📖

Date: Significance:

Thanks so much for ...

1.

2.

3.

Good things happened yesterday ...

Action I'm taking to make this day count:

Affirmation I'm putting on loop in my head:

Show me a sign:

It's all in the cards ...

Date: Significance:

Thanks so much for ...

1.

2.

3.

Good things happened yesterday ...

Action I'm taking to make this day count:

Affirmation I'm putting on loop in my head:

Show me a sign:

It's all in the cards ...

Date:

Significance:

Thanks so much for ...

1.

2.

3.

Good things happened yesterday ...

Action I'm taking to make this day count:

Affirmation I'm putting on loop in my head:

Show me a sign:

It's all in the cards ...

Date:

Significance:

Thanks so much for ...

1.

2.

3.

Good things happened yesterday ...

Action I'm taking to make this day count:

Affirmation I'm putting on loop in my head:

Show me a sign:

It's all in the cards ...

Date: Significance:

Thanks so much for ...

1.

2.

3.

Good things happened yesterday ...

Action I'm taking to make this day count:

Affirmation I'm putting on loop in my head:

Show me a sign:

It's all in the cards ...

10-Day Reflection

Manifested from my intention list:

Actions that brought the biggest results:

Collect the good, and list 'em out:

Limiting thoughts, beliefs, or stories that came up:

Keep rolling and go manifest your best!

Put the judgy eyes away.

IT'S CALLED KARMA
AND NO ONE HAS TIME
FOR BAD VIBES.

Manifest Me

INTENTIONS I'M SETTING FOR THE NEXT 10 DAYS

Personal

Relationships

Career

Money

Health

Date: Significance:

Thanks so much for ...

1.

2.

3.

Good things happened yesterday ...

Action I'm taking to make this day count:

Affirmation I'm putting on loop in my head:

Show me a sign:

It's all in the cards ...

Date: Significance:

Thanks so much for ...

1.

2.

3.

Good things happened yesterday ...

Action I'm taking to make this day count:

Affirmation I'm putting on loop in my head:

Show me a sign:

It's all in the cards ...

Date: Significance:

Thanks so much for ...

1.

2.

3.

Good things happened yesterday ...

Action I'm taking to make this day count:

Affirmation I'm putting on loop in my head:

Show me a sign:

It's all in the cards ...

Date: Significance:

Thanks so much for ...

1.

2.

3.

Good things happened yesterday ...

Action I'm taking to make this day count:

Affirmation I'm putting on loop in my head:

Show me a sign:

It's all in the cards ...

Date: Significance:

Thanks so much for ...

1.

2.

3.

Good things happened yesterday ...

Action I'm taking to make this day count:

Affirmation I'm putting on loop in my head:

Show me a sign:

It's all in the cards ...

Date: _____   Significance: _____

Thanks so much for ...

1.

2.

3.

Good things happened yesterday ...

Action I'm taking to make this day count:

Affirmation I'm putting on loop in my head:

Show me a sign:

It's all in the cards ...

Date: Significance:

Thanks so much for ...

1.

2.

3.

Good things happened yesterday ...

Action I'm taking to make this day count:

Affirmation I'm putting on loop in my head:

Show me a sign:

It's all in the cards ...

Date: Significance:

Thanks so much for ...

1.

2.

3.

Good things happened yesterday ...

Action I'm taking to make this day count:

Affirmation I'm putting on loop in my head:

Show me a sign:

It's all in the cards ...

Date: Significance:

Thanks so much for ...

1.

2.

3.

Good things happened yesterday ...

Action I'm taking to make this day count:

Affirmation I'm putting on loop in my head:

Show me a sign:

It's all in the cards ...

Date:

Significance:

Thanks so much for ...

1.

2.

3.

Good things happened yesterday ...

Action I'm taking to make this day count:

Affirmation I'm putting on loop in my head:

Show me a sign:

It's all in the cards ...

10-Day Reflection

LOOK BACK, WORK THROUGH, MOVE FORWARD.

Manifested from my intention list:

Actions that brought the biggest results:

Collect the good, and list 'em out:

Limiting thoughts, beliefs, or stories that came up:

Keep rolling and go manifest your best!

Get outside.

NOTHING RECHARGES THE SOUL LIKE SUNSHINE OR JUST SOME FRESH AIR.

Manifest Me

Personal

Relationships

Career

Money

Health

Date:

Significance:

Thanks so much for ...

1.

2.

3.

Good things happened yesterday ...

Action I'm taking to make this day count:

Affirmation I'm putting on loop in my head:

Show me a sign:

It's all in the cards ...

Date: Significance:

Thanks so much for ...

1.

2.

3.

Good things happened yesterday ...

Action I'm taking to make this day count:

Affirmation I'm putting on loop in my head:

Show me a sign:

It's all in the cards ...

Date:

Significance:

Thanks so much for ...

1.

2.

3.

Good things happened yesterday ...

Action I'm taking to make this day count:

Affirmation I'm putting on loop in my head:

Show me a sign:

It's all in the cards ...

Date: Significance:

Thanks so much for ...

1.

2.

3.

Good things happened yesterday ...

Action I'm taking to make this day count:

Affirmation I'm putting on loop in my head:

Show me a sign:

It's all in the cards ...

Date:

Significance:

Thanks so much for ...

1.

2.

3.

Good things happened yesterday ...

Action I'm taking to make this day count:

Affirmation I'm putting on loop in my head:

Show me a sign:

It's all in the cards ...

Date:

Significance:

Thanks so much for ...

1.

2.

3.

Good things happened yesterday ...

Action I'm taking to make this day count:

Affirmation I'm putting on loop in my head:

Show me a sign:

It's all in the cards ...

Date: Significance:

Thanks so much for ...
1.
2.
3.

Good things happened yesterday ...

Action I'm taking to make this day count:

Affirmation I'm putting on loop in my head:

Show me a sign:

It's all in the cards ...

Date: Significance:

Thanks so much for ...
1.
2.
3.

Good things happened yesterday ...

Action I'm taking to make this day count:

Affirmation I'm putting on loop in my head:

Show me a sign:

It's all in the cards ...

Date: Significance:

Thanks so much for ...

1.

2.

3.

Good things happened yesterday ...

Action I'm taking to make this day count:

Affirmation I'm putting on loop in my head:

Show me a sign:

It's all in the cards ...

Date: Significance:

Thanks so much for ...

1.

2.

3.

Good things happened yesterday ...

Action I'm taking to make this day count:

Affirmation I'm putting on loop in my head:

Show me a sign:

It's all in the cards ...

10-Day Reflection

LOOK BACK, WORK THROUGH, MOVE FORWARD.

Manifested from my intention list:

Actions that brought the biggest results:

Collect the good, and list 'em out:

Limiting thoughts, beliefs, or stories that came up:

Keep rolling and go manifest your best!

You can have it all.

**IN CASE YOU NEEDED
PERMISSION. THERE.**

Manifest Me

INTENTIONS I'M SETTING FOR THE NEXT 10 DAYS

Personal

Relationships

Career

Money

Health

Date: Significance:

Thanks so much for ...

1.

2.

3.

Good things happened yesterday ...

Action I'm taking to make this day count:

Affirmation I'm putting on loop in my head:

Show me a sign:

It's all in the cards ...

Date: Significance:

Thanks so much for ...

1.

2.

3.

Good things happened yesterday ...

Action I'm taking to make this day count:

Affirmation I'm putting on loop in my head:

Show me a sign:

It's all in the cards ...

Date: Significance:

Thanks so much for ...

1.

2.

3.

Good things happened yesterday ...

Action I'm taking to make this day count:

Affirmation I'm putting on loop in my head:

Show me a sign:

It's all in the cards ...

☐ 🧴   ☐ 👟   ☐ ✏️   ☐ ☯️   ☐ 📖

Date:

Significance:

Thanks so much for ...

1.

2.

3.

Good things happened yesterday ...

Action I'm taking to make this day count:

Affirmation I'm putting on loop in my head:

Show me a sign:

It's all in the cards ...

Date: Significance:

Thanks so much for ...

1.

2.

3.

Good things happened yesterday ...

Action I'm taking to make this day count:

Affirmation I'm putting on loop in my head:

Show me a sign:

It's all in the cards ...

Date: Significance:

Thanks so much for ...

1.

2.

3.

Good things happened yesterday ...

Action I'm taking to make this day count:

Affirmation I'm putting on loop in my head:

Show me a sign:

It's all in the cards ...

Date: Significance:

Thanks so much for ...

1.

2.

3.

Good things happened yesterday ...

Action I'm taking to make this day count:

Affirmation I'm putting on loop in my head:

Show me a sign:

It's all in the cards ...

Date: Significance:

Thanks so much for ...

1.

2.

3.

Good things happened yesterday ...

Action I'm taking to make this day count:

Affirmation I'm putting on loop in my head:

Show me a sign:

It's all in the cards ...

Date: Significance:

Thanks so much for …

1.

2.

3.

Good things happened yesterday …

Action I'm taking to make this day count:

Affirmation I'm putting on loop in my head:

Show me a sign:

It's all in the cards …

Date:

Significance:

Thanks so much for ...

1.

2.

3.

Good things happened yesterday ...

Action I'm taking to make this day count:

Affirmation I'm putting on loop in my head:

Show me a sign:

It's all in the cards ...

10-Day Reflection

LOOK BACK, WORK THROUGH, MOVE FORWARD.

Manifested from my intention list:

Actions that brought the biggest results:

Collect the good, and list 'em out:

Limiting thoughts, beliefs, or stories that came up:

Keep rolling and go manifest your best!

Lean
on
others.

ASK FOR HELP.
DELEGATE.
SHARE THE LOAD.

Manifest Me

INTENTIONS I'M SETTING FOR THE NEXT 10 DAYS

Personal

Relationships

Career

Money

Health

Date: Significance:

Thanks so much for ...

1.

2.

3.

Good things happened yesterday ...

Action I'm taking to make this day count:

Affirmation I'm putting on loop in my head:

Show me a sign:

It's all in the cards ...

Date:

Significance:

Thanks so much for ...

1.

2.

3.

Good things happened yesterday ...

Action I'm taking to make this day count:

Affirmation I'm putting on loop in my head:

Show me a sign:

It's all in the cards ...

Date: _____ Significance: _____

Thanks so much for ...

1.

2.

3.

Good things happened yesterday ...

Action I'm taking to make this day count:

Affirmation I'm putting on loop in my head:

Show me a sign:

It's all in the cards ...

Date: Significance:

Thanks so much for ...

1.

2.

3.

Good things happened yesterday ...

Action I'm taking to make this day count:

Affirmation I'm putting on loop in my head:

Show me a sign:

It's all in the cards ...

Date: Significance:

Thanks so much for ...

1.

2.

3.

Good things happened yesterday ...

Action I'm taking to make this day count:

Affirmation I'm putting on loop in my head:

Show me a sign:

It's all in the cards ...

☐ 🍶   ☐ 👟   ☐ ✏️   ☐ ☯️   ☐ 📖

Date: _____ Significance: _____

Thanks so much for ...

1.

2.

3.

Good things happened yesterday ...

Action I'm taking to make this day count:

Affirmation I'm putting on loop in my head:

Show me a sign:

It's all in the cards ...

☐ 🖊 ☐ 👟 ☐ ✏️ ☐ ☯ ☐ 📖

Date:

Significance:

Thanks so much for ...

1.

2.

3.

Good things happened yesterday ...

Action I'm taking to make this day count:

Affirmation I'm putting on loop in my head:

Show me a sign:

It's all in the cards ...

Date: Significance:

Thanks so much for ...

1.

2.

3.

Good things happened yesterday ...

Action I'm taking to make this day count:

Affirmation I'm putting on loop in my head:

Show me a sign:

It's all in the cards ...

Date: Significance:

Thanks so much for ...

1.

2.

3.

Good things happened yesterday ...

Action I'm taking to make this day count:

Affirmation I'm putting on loop in my head:

Show me a sign:

It's all in the cards ...

Date: Significance:

Thanks so much for ...

1.

2.

3.

Good things happened yesterday ...

Action I'm taking to make this day count:

Affirmation I'm putting on loop in my head:

Show me a sign:

It's all in the cards ...

10-Day Reflection

Manifested from my intention list:

Actions that brought the biggest results:

Collect the good, and list 'em out:

Limiting thoughts, beliefs, or stories that came up:

Keep rolling and go manifest your best!

It's all an experiment.

**THE MORE YOU TRY,
THE MORE YOU LEARN.**

Manifest Me

INTENTIONS I'M SETTING FOR THE NEXT 10 DAYS

Personal

Relationships

Career

Money

Health

Date:

Significance:

Thanks so much for ...

1.

2.

3.

Good things happened yesterday ...

Action I'm taking to make this day count:

Affirmation I'm putting on loop in my head:

Show me a sign:

It's all in the cards ...

Date: Significance:

Thanks so much for ...

1.

2.

3.

Good things happened yesterday ...

Action I'm taking to make this day count:

Affirmation I'm putting on loop in my head:

Show me a sign:

It's all in the cards ...

Date: Significance:

Thanks so much for ...

1.

2.

3.

Good things happened yesterday ...

Action I'm taking to make this day count:

Affirmation I'm putting on loop in my head:

Show me a sign:

It's all in the cards ...

Date:

Significance:

Thanks so much for ...

1.

2.

3.

Good things happened yesterday ...

Action I'm taking to make this day count:

Affirmation I'm putting on loop in my head:

Show me a sign:

It's all in the cards ...

Date: Significance:

Thanks so much for ...

1.

2.

3.

Good things happened yesterday ...

Action I'm taking to make this day count:

Affirmation I'm putting on loop in my head:

Show me a sign:

It's all in the cards ...

Date: Significance:

Thanks so much for ...

1.

2.

3.

Good things happened yesterday ...

Action I'm taking to make this day count:

Affirmation I'm putting on loop in my head:

Show me a sign:

It's all in the cards ...

Date: Significance:

Thanks so much for ...

1.

2.

3.

Good things happened yesterday ...

Action I'm taking to make this day count:

Affirmation I'm putting on loop in my head:

Show me a sign:

It's all in the cards ...

☐ 🍾 ☐ 👟 ☐ ✏️ ☐ ☯️ ☐ 📖

Date:

Significance:

Thanks so much for ...

1.

2.

3.

Good things happened yesterday ...

Action I'm taking to make this day count:

Affirmation I'm putting on loop in my head:

Show me a sign:

It's all in the cards ...

Date: Significance:

Thanks so much for ...

1.

2.

3.

Good things happened yesterday ...

Action I'm taking to make this day count:

Affirmation I'm putting on loop in my head:

Show me a sign:

It's all in the cards ...

☐ 🧴   ☐ 👟   ☐ ✏️   ☐ ☯   ☐ 📖

Date: Significance:

Thanks so much for ...

1.

2.

3.

Good things happened yesterday ...

Action I'm taking to make this day count:

Affirmation I'm putting on loop in my head:

Show me a sign:

It's all in the cards ...

10-Day Reflection

LOOK BACK, WORK THROUGH, MOVE FORWARD.

Manifested from my intention list:

Actions that brought the biggest results:

Collect the good, and list 'em out:

Limiting thoughts, beliefs, or stories that came up:

Keep rolling and go manifest your best!

Time to throw yourself a praise-parade!

YOU'VE JUST COMPLETED SIX MONTHS OF A 5-MINUTE MINDSET ROUTINE!

ORDER A NEW MIND HUSTLE JOURNAL, AND CONTINUE TO MANIFEST YOUR BEST!

Meet Rachel

BALANCING CAREER, MARRIAGE, AND MOTHERHOOD
OF THREE, RACHEL THOMAS CREATED HER BRAND,
MIND HUSTLE, TO HELP PEOPLE WORLDWIDE FIND
AN ENERGETIC BALANCE TO THEIR GRIND AND
ALIGN WITH THEIR BEST SELVES.

RACHEL LOVES TALKING ALL THINGS MINDSET ON
HER PODCAST, HUSTLE VS. FLOW, AND LIVES TO BE
YOUR BIGGEST CHEERLEADER!

Printed in the United States
By Bookmasters